Getting Started With the Internet

An Easy and Practical Guide for Teachers

by Peter Levy

SCHOLASTIC
PROFESSIONAL BOOKS

NEW YORK • TORONTO • LONDON • AUCKLAND • SYDNEY
MEXICO CITY • NEW DELHI • HONG KONG

Cover design by Holly Grundon
Cover illustrations by Sally Vitsky
Interior design by Solutions by Design, Inc.
Interior illustrations by Mike Moran

Yahooligans screenshots (pages 29–31) reproduced with permission of Yahoo! Inc. © 2000 by Yahoo! Inc.
YAHOO! and the YAHOO! logo are trademarks of Yahoo! Inc.

AOL and Netscape software images © 1999 by America Online, Inc. and Netscape Communications Corporation, respectively. Used with permission.

ISBN 0-439-14114-1

Table of Contents

Introduction

Take a deep breath. Now get ready to take the plunge.

Would you recognize a URL if it sneaked up and bit you on the ankle? Do you own a modem that's still in the original box? Have you forgotten your own e-mail address? Have you seen a little bit of the Internet and still don't understand what all the fuss is about? Or do you use the Internet at home, but aren't sure how to make it part of your classroom? If you answered yes to any of these questions, then this book is for you.

Virtually every school in America has at least one connection to the Internet. And with an estimated 13 million American kids accessing the Internet by 2003, it's time you knew more about the Internet than (or at least as much as) your students. This step-by-step tour will expose you to the exciting possibilities the Internet offers. It will teach you the essential vocabulary and show you exactly how to use the Internet for all the things you really want to do: send e-mail, find information on the World Wide Web, connect with other educators and classrooms around the world, and much more. In addition, this book will point you to some of the best places to get started with your exploration. You'll discover that the range of material on the Internet fulfills the promise: "There's something for everyone."

To give you a sense of what's possible with the Internet, let's follow a single user through a busy day and see some of the reasons she goes online. Then we'll go through each area and teach you how *you* can use that part of the Internet yourself.

*Janice is a reading specialist in Massachusetts. She's new to the Internet, but she's learned a lot very quickly. In the morning when she arrives at school, Jan checks her **e-mail** and sends a note back to her cousin in New York. During her morning class, Jan's students want to learn more about anteaters, so together they go **online** and **search** for pictures and information. In the afternoon, her class goes to the computer lab where her students correspond with another classroom in Russia as part of a world-studies unit. After school, Jan goes to a **Web site** and finds activity sheets for a lesson she is planning for the next day. She **downloads** and prints them. Later, Jan reads the e-mail that arrived from an online **discussion group** and writes back to share her experience teaching children with dyslexia.*

Wow! All that on your computer screen? It's true that you may never use the Internet to do all of these things in a single day. But after a while, you may discover that, like Jan, you use the Internet to communicate and access all kinds of information.

Whether you're a sixth-grade math teacher whose students are studying the euro, a school-library media specialist who's looking for advice from other librarians on how to set up book collections, or a fourth-grade teacher searching for information on working with students with special needs, you'll learn how the Internet can enrich and improve your teaching for you and your students.

We'll begin by reviewing key terms you may encounter on your online travels. Next, we'll go step-by-step through the process of connecting to the Internet. We'll talk about online-safety issues, and provide you with a sample Acceptable Use Policy that you can use as a template for creating one for your students. Then it's on to the specifics of the various components of the Internet: how to send e-mail, connect to discussion groups, research and save material from the World Wide Web, evaluate a Web site, and more. Finally, we'll provide you with a list of must-see Web sites to help you start panning in the world's richest information gold mine.

We've got lots to see, so let's get started!

Internet by the Numbers

According to a 1999 QED study on Internet use in public schools:

- 88.8% of schools have some connection to the Internet.

- 90.5% of schools have an Acceptable Use Policy in place.

- 75.7% of teachers report using the Internet in their teaching.

- 53.4% of teachers report using e-mail on a daily basis.

- 21% of students say that they use the Internet 1–2 hours per week.

- 92.7% of students report using the Internet for research.

Other studies of the Internet around the world also show remarkable levels of use. Recent studies show that

- 42% of all Americans, or 93 million people, went online in 1999.

- the United States accounts for more than half of the 163 million Internet users worldwide.

- 3.4 trillion e-mail messages were delivered in the U.S. in 1998. By comparison, only 107 billion pieces of first-class mail (referred to by some e-mail users as "snail mail") were delivered that same year.

- 9.4 billion e-mail messages are sent by U.S. users each day.

- 81 million Americans use e-mail.

- an estimated 1.4 billion Web pages exist today.

Experts project that there will be 7.7 billion Web pages by 2002, and about 500 million Internet users by 2003.

Net Speak

The first step to becoming an Internet pro is to understand some basic vocabulary:

@ — called an axon sign, this means "at." You'll find this symbol in all e-mail addresses.

Acceptable Use Policy (AUP) — an agreement signed by students and their parents/guardians that outlines acceptable practices for using the Internet in school

Address book — part of your e-mail program, this is a convenient way to save e-mail addresses of people to whom you write frequently

Attachment — a file sent along with an e-mail message

Bandwidth — the amount of information that can be transmitted in a given time; usually associated with the speed of a modem

Browser — a software program, such as Netscape or Internet Explorer, used to view the World Wide Web

Chat — a way to type back and forth with an individual or a group in real time

Cyberspace — a popular term for the Internet

Dedicated line — a telephone line set aside exclusively for use by your computer

Directory — a Web site that organizes information on the Internet by subject

Discussion group — a group of people with a common interest who exchange messages about a specific topic via e-mail

Domain — the address of a computer that connects to the Internet

Download — to transfer a file from the Internet (or any other computer) to your computer

E-mail — electronic mail messages

html (hypertext markup language) — the principal computer language that Web pages are written in; this defines text styles, visual layout, as well as links to other Web pages

http (hypertext transfer protocol) — the instructions your computer reads and sends to communicate on the Internet

Home page — the first page of a Web site; this often functions as a table of contents

Hyperlink or Link — a connection between one Web page and other related Web pages

Information superhighway — a popular term for the Internet

Internet or Net — literally a global "network of networks" made up of computers all over the world strung together to share information

Internet Service Provider (ISP) — a company that provides access to the Internet via a phone number or cable line

Log on/log off — to sign on or off an electronic communications system

Modem — device (sometimes inside the computer) that allows your computer to send and receive data over telephone or cable TV lines

Network — the physical connection of two or more computers through telephone lines or cables, allowing users to exchange information

Network administrator — an individual responsible for managing a computer network and its connection to the Internet

Online — common expression for being connected to the Internet

Search — to find specific information on the Internet by entering key words into a search engine

Search engine — a Web site where you can scour the Internet for relevant Web sites by entering search terms

URL (Uniform Resource Locator) — a Web address

Web site — a set of Web pages, which can range from a single page to thousands of pages

World Wide Web (WWW) — also simply called the Web, this includes millions of colorful Web pages all linked together

Connecting to the Internet

Before you can cruise along the information superhighway, you need some basic equipment to hook up to the Internet:

Computer

Any computer, Mac or PC, made since around 1990 can be used to get onto the Internet. The key difference between new and old machines is the speed at which they process and display information. New computers almost always come complete with everything you need to access the Internet.

Modem

Modems "speak computer." When someone sends you an e-mail message, the computer translates the typed message into *binary code* (computer code made of 1's and 0's), and sends it out through the modem. When the digitized message arrives at your computer, your modem translates it back into the typed format you can read.

Modems connect directly to your computer and the phone or cable-TV line. Many computers come with modems built in. Modems vary by *bandwidth*—the amount of information they can process per second. A faster modem means you can see or "load" Web pages more quickly. The standard speed for home modems right now is 56K, or 56,000 kilobits of data per second (kps). At this rate, you can send six to eight pages of typed text per second. While that sounds pretty fast, modem speeds are continually getting faster. New cable modems, for example, can transmit at speeds up to 10 Mps (megabits per second), or 1,000,000 kps. As bandwidth capacity continues to grow, you'll soon be able to view video clips over the Internet as clearly as you see them on TV.

Telephone or cable line

Many schools have a network that serves in place of a phone line. If your school does not have a network or if you are connecting from home, you'll need to access the Internet over a telephone line. Unless you have a separate phone line (called a *dedicated line*), you can't use the phone while you're on the computer.

Internet access over cable-TV lines is now becoming widely available. It requires a different type of modem but can be very fast. However, with cable modems, the more people there are that use the network in your area, the slower your connection becomes.

> ### NET TIP:
> ### Internet Hang-ups
> *If you're using the Internet at home and have call waiting, you may want to disable call waiting by dialing ✳70 (1170 on some phone systems) before you connect. This way, your Internet use will not be interrupted by an incoming call.*

An Internet Service Provider or Online Service Account

An Internet Service Provider (ISP) supplies you with special software, customer service, and a phone number that your computer calls to connect to the Internet. At school, your Internet administrator will already have picked an Internet Service Provider for you. In addition to gaining access to the Web, you will receive an e-mail account as well.

An alternative is an Online Service, such as America Online (AOL). In addition to Internet access, services like AOL provide a "gated community" of special content, tools, and discussion groups, just for subscribers. AOL also offers an easy-to-use interface and 24-hour customer service that can be especially appealing to new users.

The chart on the next page shows a partial listing of companies that provide Internet services. The service on the left provides additional content not otherwise available on the Internet. The column on the right offers direct access to the Internet.

ONLINE SERVICE	ISP
America Online www.aol.com (800) 827-6364	**AT&T Global Network** www.att.com/worldnet (800) 967-5363
	Netcom www.netcom.com (800) 638-2661
	Earthlink www.earthlink.com (800) 395-8425
	MCI Worldcom www.mciworldcom.com (800) 754-9194
	Prodigy Internet www.prodigy.com (800) PRODIGY
	MSN (Microsoft Network) www.msn.com (800) 386-5550

A Browser and E-mail Program

To go onto the Web, you will also need special free software, called a *browser,* such as Netscape or Internet Explorer. While some people use a Web browser to send and receive e-mail, you may also use a separate e-mail program such as Eudora, which is popular in many schools. See your school's technology coordinator or network administrator to find out more about the programs your school uses.

Internet Safety

I n late 1999, the Board of Education in New York City installed *filtering software* on its computer system to block students from gaining access to sites containing inappropriate material, such as sex and violence. One unintentional result: The filter denied students access to sites belonging to news outlets, policy groups, and scientific and medical organizations. Should students be prohibited from doing research on breast cancer or white-supremacy groups? The filter unleashed a firestorm of protests and opinions on both sides of the issue; students and parents complained and the American Civil Liberties Union threatened a lawsuit.

This event is just one in a series of battles over issues of Internet safety and open access to all information. Every school community needs to decide for itself how it will address the issue of Internet safety. Some schools, like those in New York City, choose to add the restrictive powers of filtering software. But as New York learned, filters may prevent your students from accessing Web sites that, in fact, have valuable information. Other schools adopt a policy in which they clearly explain the rules of appropriate and inappropriate Internet conduct, and practice a combination of student self-regulation and "over-the-shoulder" monitoring.

Internet Permission Slips

When schools get wired and add the Internet to their list of available research tools, many ask parents to sign a permission slip allowing for student access to the Internet. In addition, many schools require students to sign a contract promising to obey an outlined set of rules that cover their use of the Internet, including their online conduct. These two permission slips—with a statement of what the Internet is and how it will be used in the school setting—are known as an *Acceptable Use Policy* (AUP). See below for a sample AUP from the Bellingham, Washington, Public Schools. Feel free to use their AUP as a template for creating your own.

Whatever standards and policies you establish, it is important to publicize your policy to all members of your school community. Post the policy near your computers and send home a parent letter with the permission slip.

Personal Safety

Another significant security issue for students on the Internet is personal safety. Students should be properly advised how to handle themselves online to avoid any possible problems, such as unwanted advances from strangers. As a rule, basic common sense will go a long way to steering clear of potential pitfalls. Photocopy the safety guidelines on page 16 for each student and discuss each point with your class. Post a copy near each computer in your class, too.

SAMPLE ACCEPTABLE USE POLICY (AUP)
Internet and Electronic Mail Permission Form

THE BELLINGHAM PUBLIC SCHOOLS
We are pleased to offer students of the Bellingham Public Schools access to the district computer network for electronic mail and the Internet. To gain access to e-mail and the Internet, all students under the age of 18 must obtain parental permission and must sign and return this form to the LIBRARY MEDIA SPECIALIST. Students 18 and over may sign their own forms.

Access to e-mail and the Internet will enable students to explore thousands of libraries, databases, and bulletin boards while exchanging messages with Internet users throughout the world. Families should be warned that some material accessible via the Internet may contain items that are illegal, defamatory, inaccurate, or potentially offensive to some people. While our intent is to make Internet access available to further educational goals and objectives, students may find ways to access other materials as well. We believe that the benefits to students from access to the Internet, in the form of information resources and opportunities for collaboration, exceed any disadvantages. But ultimately, parents and guardians of minors are responsible for setting and conveying the standards that their children should follow when using media and information sources. To that end, the Bellingham Public Schools support and respect each family's right to decide whether or not to apply for access.

DISTRICT INTERNET AND E-MAIL RULES
Students are responsible for good behavior on school computer networks just as they are in a classroom or a school hallway. Communications on the network are often public in nature. General school rules for behavior and communications apply.

The network is provided for students to conduct research and communicate with others. Access to network services is given to students who agree to act in a considerate and responsible manner. Parent permis-

---

sion is required. Access is a privilege—not a right. Access entails responsibility.

Individual users of the district computer networks are responsible for their behavior and communications over those networks. It is presumed that users will comply with district standards and will honor the agreements they have signed. Beyond the clarification of such standards, the district is not responsible for restricting, monitoring, or controlling the communications of individuals utilizing the network.

Network storage areas may be treated like school lockers. Network administrators may review files and communications to maintain system integrity and ensure that users are using the system responsibly. Users should not expect that files stored on district servers will always be private.

Within reason, freedom of speech and access to information will be honored. During school, teachers of younger students will guide them toward appropriate materials. Outside of school, families bear the same responsibility for such guidance as they exercise with information sources such as television, telephones, movies, radio, and other potentially offensive media.

As outlined in Board policy and procedures on student rights and responsibilities, copies of which are available in school offices, the following are not permitted:

- Sending or displaying offensive messages or pictures
- Using obscene language
- Harassing, insulting, or attacking others
- Damaging computers, computer systems, or computer networks

- Violating copyright laws
- Using another's password
- Trespassing in another's folders, work, or files
- Intentionally wasting limited resources
- Employing the network for commercial purposes

Violations may result in a loss of access as well as other disciplinary or legal action.

USER AGREEMENT AND PARENT PERMISSION FORM – 1995

As a user of the Bellingham Public Schools computer network, I hereby agree to comply with the above stated rules—communicating over the network in a reliable fashion while honoring all relevant laws and restrictions.

Student Signature _____

As the parent or legal guardian of the minor student signing above, I grant permission for my son or daughter to access networked computer services such as electronic mail and the Internet. I understand that individuals and families may be held liable for violations. I understand that some materials on the Internet may be objectionable, but I accept responsibility for guidance of Internet use—setting and conveying standards for my daughter or son to follow when selecting, sharing, or exploring information and media.

Parent Signature _____ Date _____

Name of Student_____

School_____ Grade _____

Soc. Sec. # _____ Birth Date _____

Street Address _____

Home Telephone _____

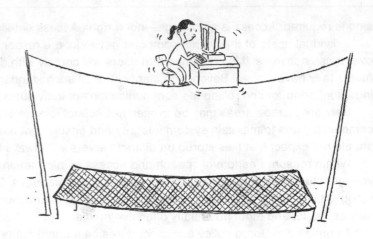

SAFETY on the NET

1. When communicating with others online, never give out personal information, such as your full name, home address, school name and address, or telephone number.

2. Do not send your picture to someone on the Internet without your parents' and/or teacher's permission.

3. Do not agree to get together with anyone you meet over the Internet without first getting your parents' and/or teacher's permission. If you do arrange to meet someone face-to-face, go with a trusted friend and meet in a public place.

4. Never respond to e-mail, chat comments, or any other messages that are hostile, inappropriate, mean, or make you feel uncomfortable in any way. If you do get such a message, tell your teacher or parent right away.

5. If you come across any information or Web site that makes you feel uncomfortable, tell your teacher or parent right away.

Getting Started With the Internet Scholastic Professional Books

New Ways to Talk

T he Internet offers many options for communicating. You can send someone a message via e-mail, join mailing lists and discussion groups, or "talk" to someone live in a chat room. Read on for more.

Electronic Mail (or E-mail)

E-mail is the most widely used part of the Internet. More than four trillion e-mail messages were delivered in the U.S. in 1999. Literally billions of e-mail messages are being sent around the world right now.

Why are so many people sending so many e-mail messages? Because it's fast, fun, and best of all, it's free. Once you log on to the Internet, you can send an e-mail message to anyone in the world who also has an e-mail account.

Your school may offer an e-mail software program, such as Eudora, or your network administrator may instruct you to send and receive mail through a Web browser. Gaggle.Net (at http://www.gaggle.net) is a popular, free e-mail service specially designed for teachers and their students. You don't need any additional hardware or software. You and your students can simply access your e-mail from any computer that has an Internet connection—at school, in the library, or at home. Best of all, Gaggle.Net has a built-in monitoring system that lets you, the teacher, have control over your students' e-mail.

If you are getting your first e-mail account through your school instead, your computer administrator will likely provide you with your e-mail address. Let's look at two e-mail addresses to understand their elements:

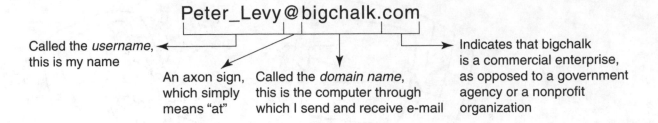

Peter_Levy@bigchalk.com

Called the *username*, this is my name

An axon sign, which simply means "at"

Called the *domain name*, this is the computer through which I send and receive e-mail

Indicates that bigchalk is a commercial enterprise, as opposed to a government agency or a nonprofit organization

Let's look at another one:

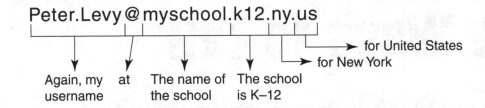

Peter.Levy@myschool.k12.ny.us

Again, my username

at

The name of the school

The school is K–12

for United States

for New York

NET TIP: What's in a Name?

The dot followed by three letters at the end of an e-mail address gives you important information about the recipient. Take a look at the various domain types:

> *.com—commercial enterprise*
>
> *.net—network service or commercial*
>
> *.gov—government*
>
> *.edu—education*
>
> *.org—organization*
>
> *.mil—military*

An address that ends with dot followed by two letters is a country indicator. For example:

> *.us—United States*
>
> *.fr—France*
>
> *.uk—United Kingdom*
>
> *.ca—Canada*
>
> *.de—Germany*
>
> *.nz—New Zealand*

After you get your e-mail address, you'll need to pick a *password*. Used for security purposes, passwords help keep your e-mail correspondence private. Select a password that's easy for you to remember and don't share it with anyone. Security experts believe that a non-word password—a combination of letters and numbers—is more secure. If you are very concerned about privacy, change your password about once a month.

Most e-mail programs operate in very similar ways. If you understand the basics of how one e-mail program works, the differences between programs are easy to figure out.

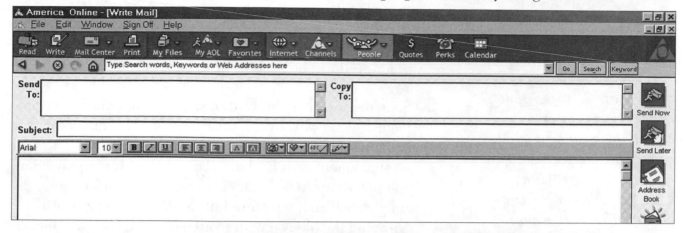

Eudora ➤

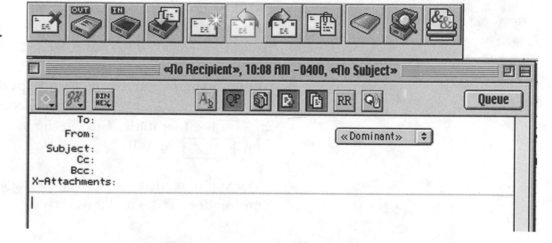

How to Write and Send E-mail (with attachments)

1. If you are using Eudora, select the **Message** tab and pull down to **New Message**. In America Online, click on the **Mail Center** icon and pull down on **Write Mail.**

2. Click on the box to the right of the word **To** and type the e-mail address of the person to whom you are writing. NOTE: Make sure you type in your recipient's address correctly. If you make a mistake, a notice will come back to you saying that your mail could not be delivered. If you want to send your message to more than one person, simply list each recipient separated by either a comma or a semicolon, depending on your e-mail program. Check the online Help files or your software manual to find out which separator to use.

3. Next, click your mouse on the box to the right of the word **Subject** or **RE** and write a brief descriptive phrase that says what the e-mail is about.

4. Now click on the body of the letter and type your message or letter. It can be as short or as long as you like.

5. Sometimes you might want to send another document or picture along with your e-mail. This is called an *attachment* and it works like paper clipping a file to your letter. To send an attachment with Eudora, click on the **Message** header and pull down **Attach Document**. In America Online, simply click on the picture button that says **Attach Files**. Now find the file you wish to attach. Once you have found the file you wish to include, click on the **Open** or the **Attach** button. The selected document or photograph will be sent piggybacked to your e-mail.

6. Most e-mail programs come with a **spell check** function to check for mispelled … er … misspelled words. The spell checker is either under **Edit** in the menu bar or is this icon [ABC✓] in AOL.

7. Once you're ready to send your message, just click the **Send** button. That's all there is to it!

Receiving E-mail

In most mail programs, retrieving e-mail is incredibly easy. Simply log on to the Internet, open your e-mail program, and enter your password. In Eudora, you may need to go under the **File** menu and select **Check Mail**. Depending on how your school's system is set up, your messages may or may not be saved on your computer. Some programs save messages automatically into your **Inbox**. You can also manually save e-mail onto your hard drive or onto a floppy disk. America Online stores messages for only a limited time before they become irretrievable, so you should download messages you want to keep. To save a message with AOL, open the message and then select **Save To Incoming Mail Drawer** under the **File** menu. Whatever system your school uses, it's always a good idea to clean up your incoming messages frequently by deleting files you don't need, or saving important messages to disk.

Replying to E-mail

To reply to an e-mail message, simply hit the **Reply** button. A new message box will open that is already addressed to the person to whom you're replying. Note that most mail programs also have a **Reply to All** option. If you are responding to an e-mail that was sent to a large group of people, using the **Reply to All** button sends your response to the entire mailing list.

Forwarding E-mail

If you receive an e-mail message that you'd like to forward to someone else, simply select the **Forward** button in AOL, or select **Forward To** from under the **Message** column in Eudora. Then type the e-mail addresses of the people to whom you would like to forward the mail and hit the **Send** button.

Creating an Address Book

To save e-mail addresses of people you write to regularly, you can create an e-mail **address book**. With an address book (also known as *contacts*), you won't need to remember the long e-mail addresses of your friends, family, and colleagues. Simply select their names from a list, and the program will automatically insert their e-mail addresses in the **To** field.

To create an address book in America Online, simply hit the **Remember Address** button and fill in the on-screen prompts. Eudora calls its address book "Nicknames." To create a list of Nicknames, select **Nicknames** from under the Window header.

NET TIP: Smileys

While online conversations can be deeply personal, it can sometimes be difficult to express mood or emotions. Over time, Internet users have created ways to add feeling to their writing. These emotions are expressed in a set of icons, called smileys *or emoticons (combining emotion with icon). Take a look at these popular smileys (turn the page sideways to see the "faces"):*

:-> or :-)	*happy*
:-<	*sad*
:- o	*surprised*
:-D	*laughing*
;-)	*winking*

NET TIP: Abbreviations

People who send e-mail have also developed a way to cut corners on some frequently used expressions. Here is a sample of some online shorthand:

BRB	*Be right back*
BTW	*By the way*
GMTA	*Great minds think alike*
IMHO	*In my humble opinion*
LOL	*Laugh out loud*
WB	*Write back*
TTFN	*Ta-ta for now!*

Mailing Lists and Discussion Groups

Now that you know how to send and receive e-mail, perhaps you're wondering to whom you are going to write. In addition to writing to friends and family, you can access a world of mailing lists, organized around a specific topic, through the Internet.

Mailing lists and *discussion groups* are forums through which people with common interests share their experience and opinions. If you are a library media specialist, you might want to check out LM_NET, a discussion group that addresses specific issues that concern K–12 librarians. Many elementary-school bilingual teachers have Bilingue-L, while those interested in children's literature participate in Childlit. Technology teachers subscribe to Computer Networking Education (CNEDUC-L). For almost any area of interest, you can usually find at least one discussion group and mailing list.

How Mailing Lists Work

Each mailing list has two e-mail addresses. One address is for subscribing and unsubscribing (putting yourself on and off the list). The other address is for communicating to the other members of the discussion group. When you send e-mail to this second address, it gets distributed to everyone else on the list. In some cases, a host moderates the list so that the discussion stays focused on the topic at hand. Many lists, however, are not moderated, which, for better or worse, allows mailing lists to be a free-flowing conversation between participants.

Joining a Mailing List

Subscribing to mailing lists is free—just send an e-mail message to the "subscription address." Leave the subject line of your message blank. In the message box type:

Subscribe <LISTNAME><Yourfirstname Yourlastname>

Of course, you would substitute your actual name for Yourfirstname Yourlastname. For example:

Subscribe CHILDLIT Peter Levy

or

Subscribe LM_NET Peter Levy

If the subscription address of a discussion group starts with "listname-request" or "Majordomo," send the following message inside your e-mail. Again, send this message to the subscription address and remember to leave the subject field blank.

A Gold Mine for Library Media Specialists

Paula Yohe, a library media specialist at the J.V. Martin Junior High in Dillon, South Carolina, searches the updated message archives of LM_NET every morning. "A variety of questions and concerns are posted daily, ranging from a problem with a specific printer to a discussion about the role of library media specialists in education," Paula explains. Paula goes to LM_NET to find lists of books that are popular with students, learn how to fix technical problems, read other media specialists' opinions about new software products, discuss censorship issues, and more. There's usually only one media specialist in a school and no one to bounce ideas off or get support from, Paula points out. She says the LM_NET is "an invaluable resource for any library professional seeking help or opinions from others in the profession."

Sub <LISTNAME>

For example:

Sub CACI or **Sub NET-HAPPENINGS**

Note that you don't include your name in this last type of mailing list. Once your mail is received, you will automatically receive a message with some basic information about the discussion group and how you can participate. Then, depending on how active the group is, you will receive something between a trickle and a deluge of e-mail from other participants in the discussion group.

If at any point you want to remove yourself from the list, you will need to unsubscribe. The process varies from list to list, but generally, you'll need to send a message with the word "unsubscribe," followed by the name of the list and your e-mail address.

Mailing List Directory

To find a mailing list of interest to you, check out the suggestions below. For a directory of mailing lists concerning education issues, look on the Web at http://ericir.syr.edu/Virtual/Listserv_Archives. For a more comprehensive directory of mailing lists on all subjects, go to http://www.liszt.com.

Bilingue-L
    Elementary Teachers of Spanish/English
    Subscription address: listserv@lists.k12.or.us
    Submission address: BILINGUE-L@lists.k12.or.us

CHILDLIT
    Children's Literature: Criticism and Theory
    Subscription address: listserv@email.rutgers.edu
    Submission address: CHILD_LIT@email.rutgers.edu

CNEDUC-L
    Computer Networking Education
    Subscription address: listserv@tamvm1.tamu.edu
    Submission address: CNEDUC-L@tamvm1.tamu.edu

ECENET-L
    Early Childhood Education/Young Children (0–8)
    Subscription address: listserv@postoffice.cso.uiuc.edu
    Submission address: ECENET-L@postoffice.cso.uiuc.edu

EDNET
    Discussion of the Educational Potential of the Internet
    Subscription address: listproc@lists.umass.edu
    Submission address: EDTECH@lists.umass.edu

ELED-L
Elementary Education
Subscription address: listserv@ksuvm.ksu.edu
Submission address: ELED-L@ksu.edu

LM_NET
School Library Media & Network Communications
Subscription address: listserv@listserv.syr.edu
Submission address: LM_NET@listserv.syr.edu

T321-L
Teaching Science in Elementary School
Subscription address: listserv@mizzou1.missouri.edu
Submission address: T321-L@mizzou1.missouri.edu

TAG-L
Talented and Gifted Education
Subscription address: listserv@listserv.nodak.edu
Submission address: TAG-L@listserv.nodak.edu

Chat

A *chat* is somewhere between a discussion group and an old-fashioned conversation. Chat is a way to type back and forth with an individual or a group in real time. Although everyone participating in a chat can type at the same time, the message from each participant appears on the screen in the order in which it is received, along with the screen name of the person who typed it. Chats take place in a "location" on the Internet called a *chat room*. Like discussion groups, chat rooms are usually focused on a particular subject. There are chat areas on many popular kids Web sites. On America Online, chat is one of the most popular activities for kids and teens.

Netiquette

As you begin to participate in online discussion groups and chats, you'll soon realize that although these groups could be a wild and chaotic free-for-all, a sense of order is somehow maintained. Over its brief 30-year history, the Internet community has developed a set of rules, sometimes called *Netiquette*, which serves as an unwritten code to maintain a positive environment for everyone. Photocopy the "Rules of the Net" on page 25 for each student and discuss each point with your class. Post a copy in your computer center, too.

RULES OF THE NET
(a.k.a. Netiquette)

1. Treat others with courtesy and respect.

2. Never use inappropriate language.

3. WRITING IN ALL CAPS IS CONSIDERED SCREAMING!

4. Keep your communication direct and to the point. (Some people pay for their Internet connection by the hour. Do your best to conserve everyone's time and money.)

5. Make sure your comments are relevant to the topic at hand.

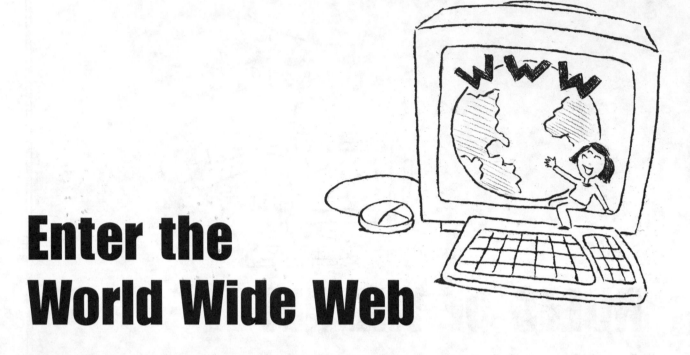

Enter the
World Wide Web

More and more people are turning to the *World Wide Web* to find all sorts of information. Although technically only part of the Internet, the World Wide Web (or simply "the Web") is what most people mean when they talk about the Internet. When you hear someone talk about "*surfing the net*," that person means clicking from Web page to Web page.

A *Web page* includes text, pictures, animation, and even sound and video at a specific location on the Internet. A *Web site* is a collection of these pages.

What makes the Web so powerful? Web pages contain *hyperlinks* or *links* that connect one Web site to other related pages. Hyperlinks are easy to recognize because they are usually underlined or different-color text, or clickable pictures or icons. When you click on the link, you jump to another page containing more specific or related information. Millions and millions of pages are all directly or indirectly linked together in one enormous Web.

Address, Please!

Each Web page has an address, called a URL (Uniform Resource Locator). Here are the different parts of a URL:

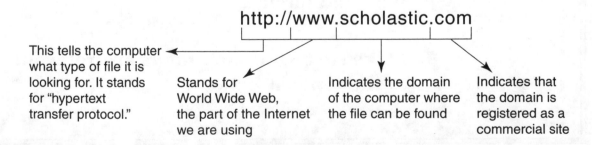

http://www.scholastic.com

This tells the computer what type of file it is looking for. It stands for "hypertext transfer protocol."

Stands for World Wide Web, the part of the Internet we are using

Indicates the domain of the computer where the file can be found

Indicates that the domain is registered as a commercial site

As with e-mail addresses, URLs have a wide range of endings: .com, .edu, .org, .gov, .mil, and .net. (*See NET TIP: What's in a Name?, page 18.*)

When you type in a URL, make sure you include the full, correct address. Internet addresses are unforgiving. If you miss one letter or type your slashes the wrong way, you'll get an error message. If you're having trouble, double-check that you've typed the URL correctly.

Anatomy of a Browser

Internet Explorer 4.01

Netscape Communicator™

To view a Web page, you need special, free software called a *browser*. Netscape and Internet Explorer are the two most-popular Web browsers.

To go onto the Web, double-click on your browser. On your desktop, the icon will look like one of the top two symbols at left. If you're logged on to America Online, simply click on the "Go to the Web" icon to launch your browser.

Understanding the features of your browser can make managing the Web much easier. Let's take a look at the functions of the different buttons on the toolbar.

1. The **Back** button takes you to the last page you visited.

2. If you have used the Back button already, the **Forward** button returns you to the previous page you were viewing.

3. **Reload** or **Refresh** loads the page you're on. Click this button if the page doesn't load properly.

4. **Home** takes you to your default page. This is the page that opens automatically when you launch your browser. (*See NET TIP: Changing Your Browser's Default Page, page 28.*)

5. **Print** sends the Web page on your screen to the printer.

6. **Security** shows security information about the page, such as encryption, passwords, etc.

7. **Stop** stops the current page from loading.

8. **Location** or **Address** is where you type in the URL of a Web site.

> ### NET TIP: Changing your Browser's Default Page
>
>
>
> *Many people have particular Web pages that they visit again and again. You can set your browser to automatically load this page each time you open up your browser or hit the **Home** button on your toolbar.*
>
> *If you are using Netscape 4.0, click the **Edit** menu, then click **Preferences**. Select **Navigator** and replace the **Home Page** field. On Netscape 3.0, go to **Options** and pull down the **General Preferences** menu. There, you'll see a box where you can change your default home page.*
>
> *If you are using Internet Explorer on your PC, simply right-click on the **IE** logo on your desktop, then pull down and left-click on the word **Properties**. There, you'll be able to change the default home page.*

Search Engines and Directories

There are several different ways of finding information on the Web. One way is to request help from other Internet users who may have the information you need, or who know where to find it. Another way is to explore the Web on your own with either a search engine or a directory.

A *search engine* is a type of Web site that scours the Internet for other Web sites that match the key words you type in. A *directory* is a Web site that organizes huge numbers of other Web sites in hierarchical order by subject. Many sites offer both ways of searching. Let's take a look at each tool to understand its strengths and weaknesses.

With a search engine, you enter some key words that are relevant to your subject. For example, let's say your class is studying the animals of Asia. We'll go to the search engine AltaVista to search for Siberian tiger.

Find this: `Siberian Tiger` **Search**

Type in the words "Siberian tiger" into the search box. A list of sites will come up on the *search results* page. Each site on the list includes a title and a brief description of what the site is about. Click on the title (the underlined or different-color text) to go to that site. Use the Back button on the browser to return to your search results page.

Our search results for Siberian tigers brought back more than 1,900 sites (also called *hits*). Going through all of those sites would be a lot of work! Not to worry. Search engines usually rank sites by the percentage of correlation to your terms. That means you'll find the most relevant sites in the top 10 to 20 results.

As you can see, search engines are very fast and search through thousands and thousands of sites. If you're searching for something clear and discrete and you simply want to find the needle in the haystack, a search engine is the way to go. The main drawback is that sometimes you get huge lists of results that may include lots of irrelevant Web sites.

With a directory, however, you begin at the broadest category and drill down until you get to exactly what you're looking for. Let's use the Yahooligans directory to do the same search for Siberian tigers.

1. Begin on the home page and click on Animals under the category of Science & Nature.

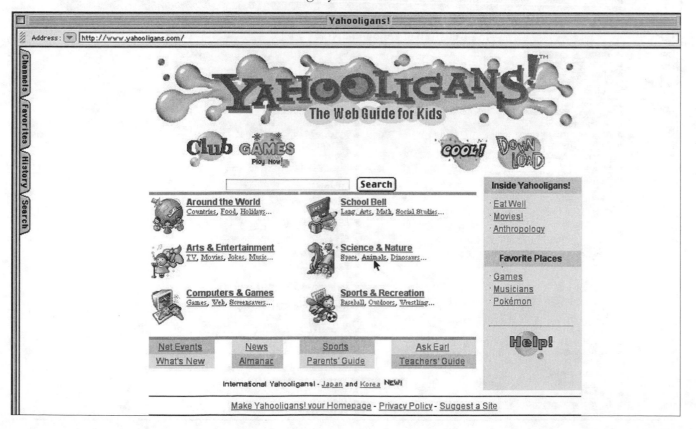

2. Next click on Mammals.

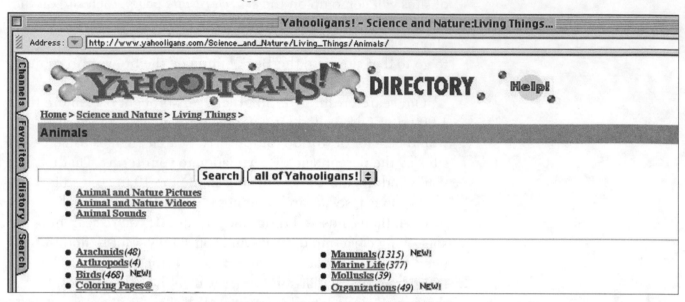

3. From this list, select Tigers.

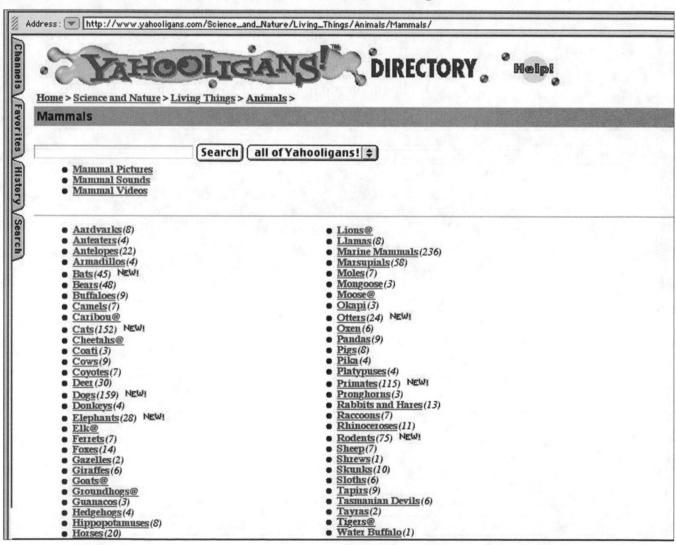

4. Click on Siberian Tigers.

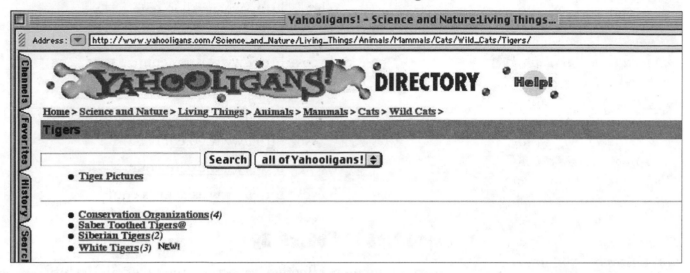

5. You got two sites, specifically about Siberian Tigers.

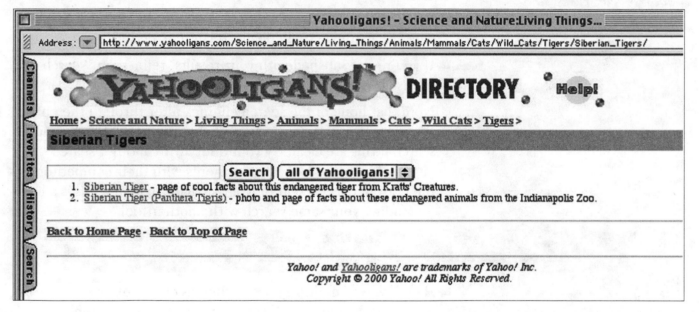

Directories have two significant benefits over search engines. First, they are organized by subject matter, so you can see yourself getting closer and closer to your exact subject as you progress. Second, because the process involves drilling down to greater specificity, your final list of Web pages is usually a highly concentrated list of relevant pages. Instead of the 1,900-plus sites spouted by the search engine (not all of which were useful), the directory found two targeted, high-quality sites.

Below are some of the most popular search engines and directories. Each one has a slightly different method for conducting searches. Experiment with several until you find the one that works best for you. Type one of these addresses into your

NET TIP:
Yahoo! for Kids

If you are searching with your kids in class, check out Yahooligans (http://www.yahooligans.com)— a directory and search engine designed just for kids in grades K–8, and links only to appropriate sites. In addition to being a "kid-centric" directory and search tool, Yahooligans organizes content under popular areas such as sports, celebrities, and games.

browser and hit the Return or Enter key on your keyboard.

Yahoo!	http://www.yahoo.com
Yahooligans	http://www.yahooligans.com
Lycos	http://www.lycos.com
AltaVista	http://www.altavista.com
Homework Central	http://www.homeworkcentral.com
Go	http://www.go.com
Excite	http://www.excite.com
Ask Jeeves	http://www.askjeeves.com

Some Tips to Search By

Learning the most effective ways to search takes time. Until then, follow these tips for searching:

- Spelling counts! If you're not getting any meaningful results, check that you've spelled your terms correctly.

- If you're not satisfied with your results, refine your search terms and try again.

- Note that none of the search engines filter through the entire Internet. If you're not finding what you need but think your search terms are clear, try your query with another search engine. Most sites have arrangements with their competitors— the bottom of your search results page usually includes a link to conduct your same search with another tool.

Other Search Engines
Alta Vista - dot com directory - GoTo.com - HotBot - Infoseek - deja.com - More...

- If you type in multiple words, such as *classroom management*, most search engines will return pages that have either "classroom" or "management" in them. If you want to restrict your search to only those pages that contain all words, place quotes around the words: "classroom management." Or, use the + sign between your terms: classroom+management.

- Most search engines are based on *Boolean logic,* which works to expand or restrict the number of results that are returned for your search. Here's the idea in a nutshell:

  - Placing an "and" between search terms yields results that contain both or all words.

  - Placing an "or" between terms will bring back results that contain either word.

• Placing a "not" between terms will bring back documents about the first term, but not the second.

▣ Sometimes when you click on one of the sites listed in your search results, you may receive a message, such as Server Busy, DNS Error, or Error 404 Not Found. "Server Busy" simply means that the site can't allow you entry at that time. Try again in a few minutes. A DNS error or Error 404 message indicates that the site you're looking for isn't where it's supposed to be. The computer that hosts the site may be temporarily off or under repair. It's also possible that the site is just gone, as is sometimes the nature of the Internet.

Finding Professional Resources

You can find lots of curricular and professional resources on the Web. Educators often post their lesson plans, and many companies make curriculum or professional-development materials available, often free of charge. This wealth of professional resources can be especially beneficial to new teachers, who need to find effective ideas and strategies, quickly. "The Web is a great resource for a new teacher," says Brandon Alvarez, a first-year teacher at the Brooklyn New School in Brooklyn, New York. Brandon searches through the professional resources on www.bigchalk.com and www.enchantedlearning.com to get lesson plans and to learn new techniques for classroom management. "The Web allows me to look up almost every situation that I've faced as a first-year teacher," he says.

Evaluating a Web Site

The greatest challenge to students using the Internet is sorting through the tremendous amount of information they find on the Net, says Cornelia Brunner, associate director of the Center for Children and Technology/EDC. "Kids have never before been exposed to information in such variety—not only by subject but in quality," she says. Brunner argues that critical-thinking skills become increasingly important in wading through all the information out there. "Kids need to develop skills to figure out how to eliminate information. They need to learn how to say, 'I don't even have to look at that, that's not useful,' and then to ask, 'What's missing?'"

To help students learn how to evaluate the Web sites, photocopy the Web Site Evaluation Sheet and Criteria on pages 37–38.

Encourage students to determine the usefulness of a Web site you and your class visit. You can then post the best Web sites you've seen on a bulletin board.

Bookmarks and Favorites

When you find a site you like, it's useful to "tag" it so you can easily return another time. Netscape refers to this way of saving Web addresses as **Bookmarks**, while AOL and Internet Explorer call them **Favorites**. This saves you the hassle of remembering a long address or the trail of links that got you to the site in the first place. Marking pages for your students is a valuable time-saver, allowing them to go directly to the sites you've preselected and begin their work.

How to Set Bookmarks and Favorites

1. If you're using Netscape, click on **Bookmarks** on the menu bar, then select **Add Bookmark**. If you're using Internet Explorer, select **Add To Favorites** by clicking on **Favorites** on the menu bar. In America Online, click on the heart icon in the upper right-hand corner of the screen. Once you set a Bookmark or Favorite, it goes into a list in the order created and is available from the menu bar.

2. If you bookmark many sites, the list can quickly become long and unmanageable. To help organize your bookmarks, browsers let you create folders (and even folders within the folders). In Netscape, select **Bookmarks** from under the Navigator icon in the menu bar. Next, under the **File** menu, select **New Folder**. In Internet Explorer, select

NET TIP:
Double-checking
Your Bookmarks

If you choose to create Bookmarks for your class, check to make sure the sites are still available before a group of students comes to use them. Many Web sites are frequently moved and renamed. Some change addresses and others just disappear altogether. Confirming that your bookmarks are still "live" will save your students frustration and keep your class time focused on your intended activity.

Organize Favorites from the **Favorites** on the menu bar. Then click on the icon to the right to create a new folder.

3. Name the folder so that it will be easy for future users to access. Some teachers choose to name the folders for the subject area, such as "evolutionary biology." Others label folders for the intended user, such as "3rd period."

4. Once you label the folder, you can click and drag all of the related bookmarks into it. The next time users come to that computer, they can click on the folder you created and find the bookmarks inside.

5. To delete a Bookmark or Favorite that you no longer want, simply return to **Bookmarks** or **Organize Favorites**, select the site you wish to remove, and hit the **Delete** button.

Using Bookmarks in the Classroom

Scott Bales, a fourth-grade teacher at Rorimer Elementary in La Puenta, California, uses the Web as an extension to his class's exploration of the importance of water to California's environment. Scott selects 8 of his 30 students to work on the Web while the rest of the class engages in group activities. The selected students work in pairs for 45-minute blocks. Each duo is assigned one of California's four regions— Mountains and Desert, the Coastal Range, the Coast, and the Central Valley. Scott bookmarks the relevant sites for the unit. "The students go to the Web sites, decide what's important, print selected pages, and produce a poster and an accompanying report," Scott explains.

Scott believes it's critical to keep the use of the Internet focused on what the whole class is working on. "If you don't tie the Internet activity directly to curriculum, you've lost the point of why you did it."

Copying and Saving Text and Images

Students may need to copy and save text and images from Web sites to use in their own projects. To copy text, click and hold down the mouse (the left side if you're on a PC) and drag it over the text you want to copy. Then select **Copy** from under the **Edit** menu at the top of your screen. Next, open your word processor, such as Microsoft Word. From under the **Edit** menu, click on **Paste** and the text will appear.

Copying images is even easier. On the Mac, click and hold down the mouse on the image you want to copy. From the menu that appears, select **Save This Image As**. You can then rename the image and save it on your computer. On the PC, right-click on the image and pull down on **Save Picture As**.… Then select the location where you want the image to be saved.

Citing Your Sources

It's important to teach students that information and images taken from the Internet must be treated as any other source—credit must be given. Here's one way to cite sources:

WWW Resources

1. Author's name (Last, First) or name of organization
2. Title of Web site in *italics*, or with quotes if newspaper, magazine, or encyclopedia article
3. URL (http://) with brackets [ ]
4. Date you accessed the Web site

> Example:
> Endangered Species Fund of Canada. *The Savannah of Southern Ontario*.
> [http://www.junglecatworld.com/junglecatworld.html]
> December 1, 1999.

E-mail

1. Writer's name (Last, First)
2. Subject line with quotation marks
3. Writer's e-mail address (<u>username@…</u>) in brackets [ ]
4. Date the e-mail was sent

> Example:
> Levy, Peter "Information on Siberian Tigers"
> [<u>Peter_Levy@bigchalk.com</u>] December 1, 1999.

Name: _____

Web Site (URL): _____

Web Site Evaluation Sheet

Rate each of the criteria on a scale of 0 to 5, with 5 as the highest possible score.
See next page for explanation about each criterion.

CRITERIA	SCORE					
Accuracy	0	1	2	3	4	5
Authorship	0	1	2	3	4	5
Balance	0	1	2	3	4	5
Comprehensiveness	0	1	2	3	4	5
Currency	0	1	2	3	4	5
Ease of Navigation	0	1	2	3	4	5
Legibility	0	1	2	3	4	5
Speed	0	1	2	3	4	5

TOTAL (from 0 to 40): _____

Would you recommend this site? Why or why not?

_____

_____

_____

_____

_____

Comments:

_____

_____

_____

_____

Criteria for Evaluating Web Sites

Accuracy— Is the content on the site accurate? If the site features notable experts, there is a good chance that the information is reliable. For example, if you are studying space, NASA is a reliable source of information.

Authorship— Is the name of the individual or group that created the site clearly stated? Is it possible to e-mail them if you have questions or comments, or if you find problems?

Balance— Is the site written objectively? What might the authors' intentions be for creating the site? (Tip: You can gather a lot of information about the authors' possible biases by the links they provide.)

Comprehensiveness— Does the site have a clear focus and cover the subject in sufficient depth? For the areas the site doesn't address, does it have links to other sites that provide the missing information?

Currency— Is the information on the site current? Does this affect the quality of the information? (Tip: If the subject matter is time-sensitive, look for clues that indicate when it was last updated. If the home page of a site is touting results of the November election in February, you should probably keep searching.)

Ease of Navigation— Is the information you want easy to find? Is the content organized into meaningful categories? Does the way you navigate the site (link from one part to the next) make sense?

Legibility— Is the text legible? Is the site easy on your eyes?

Speed— Is the site designed so that it loads on your computer quickly? (A Web page that is filled with pictures is sometimes called a "heavy page." Waiting for these pages to load can be frustrating.)

Getting Started With the Internet   Scholastic Professional Books

Internet Activities

The Internet opens a new world of experiences, resources, and collaboration for your students. A wealth of sites designed just for kids provides online expeditions to exotic places, interactive learning games, and connections with experts—just to name a few. Here are some classroom Internet activities to get you started and link students to a new way of learning.

ACTIVITY 1

Send a Postcard From the Zoo! - ∘∘∘

SUBJECT AREAS: Science, Language Arts

OVERVIEW: Take a virtual class trip to the zoo. Students will "visit" their favorite animals, then send a postcard with a fun fact about the animals.

TO DO:

1. Brainstorm animals that can be found in the zoo and make a list on the board.

2. Divide the class into groups of two and assign each pair one animal. Have them visit the zoo Web sites on the following page. Their mission: Learn more about their animal at the virtual zoo.

3. Encourage students to take notes about their animal, such as its diet, natural habitat, and distinct characteristics.

4. After they've explored one or two zoo sites and collected information about their animals, direct students to one of the "Electronic Postcards" sites. Ask them to browse the postcards for one that features an animal they visited at the zoo.

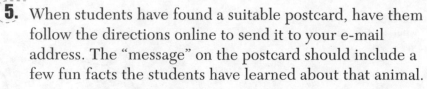

5. When students have found a suitable postcard, have them follow the directions online to send it to your e-mail address. The "message" on the postcard should include a few fun facts the students have learned about that animal.

6. Invite students to join you as you check your e-mail box for each pair's electronic postcard. Print the postcards and hang them on the bulletin board.

SUGGESTED SITES...

Zoos and Animal Parks

San Diego Zoo
http://www.sandiegozoo.org/apps/animals

Zoo Atlanta
http://www.zooatlanta.org/anim.html

Birmingham Zoo
http://www.birminghamzoo.com/animals

Sea World/Busch Gardens
http://www.seaworld.org/animal_bytes/animal_bytes.html

Electronic Postcards

San Diego Zoo Postcards
http://www.sandiegozoo.org/postcards/send.php3

Lions and Tigers Electronic Cards
http://www.lionsandtigers.scotland.net/flash/trading/cards.htm

....

ACTIVITY 2

Ask a Scientist .... ◦ ◦ ◦

SUBJECT AREAS: Science

OVERVIEW: Ever wish you could bring an astronomer, geologist, or dinosaur expert into the classroom to answer those questions only experts could know? Well, you can! You'll find many sites online with real scientists available to answer questions from your students.

TO DO:

1. During your next science unit, keep a list of kids' questions on your bulletin board.

2. When you've collected 10–15 questions, review the list with your class. Could any of the questions be answered by doing research in the library or on the Internet? For example, you could find the answer to the question "How far away is Pluto?" on many Web sites. (A great place to start research is Scholastic.com's Web Guide at http://teacher.scholastic.com/webguide/index.htm.) Place an "R" (for research) next to these questions.

3. Divide students into small groups and assign each group a research question.

4. When each group has had an opportunity to find the answer to their assigned question, have them present the answers to the class. What else did they discover in their research?

5. When students successfully answer a question, cross it off the bulletin board. If a group could not find an answer, erase the "R" next to the question.

6. Review the remaining questions on the bulletin board and have students discuss which two or three questions they'd most like answered. Depending on the theme of your unit, you can choose one of the ask-an-expert sites on the following page to visit and ask your questions.

7. Before students submit their questions, make sure they search the archive of questions that have already been answered. (In most cases, scientists will not answer repeat questions.) If their question has not been answered, send the question to the scientist. Review students' letters for correct grammar and spelling, and make sure that students submit appropriate questions.

8. Check the site to see if scientists will e-mail answers or post them directly on the Web site. Assign a student to check the site or e-mail in a few days to see if an answer has been posted or sent. (Scientists usually take between a few days to a couple of weeks to answer a question.) Encourage students to be patient—scientists frequently answer hundreds of questions each week!

9. Once an answer has been posted, have students present it to the class and print out the exchange to hang on the bulletin board. Continue the activity throughout the year,

and you'll have a bulletin board filled with answers and comments from real scientists!

SITES TO GET STARTED..

Ask-a-Geologist
http://walrus.wr.usgs.gov/docs/ask-a-ge.html

Ask Dr. Universe (General Science)
http://www.wsu.edu/DrUniverse

Brainium
http://www.brainium.com

Mad Scientist Network
http://www.madsci.org

Ask an Earth Scientist
http://www.soest.hawaii.edu/GG/ASK/askanerd.html

How Things Work: The Physics of Everyday Life
http://rabi.phys.virginia.edu/HTW

Space Team Online
http://quest.arc.nasa.gov/space/ask/question.html

Yahooligans' "Ask a Scientist" sites
http://www.yahooligans.com/Science_and_Nature/
Homework_Help/Ask_a_Scientist

....

ACTIVITY 3

Take Part in a National Poll

SUBJECT AREAS: Social Studies, Math

OVERVIEW: Where do your students stand on today's hot issues? Do their opinions reflect those of other kids their age? Through online polls and surveys, students can share their thoughts and opinions with kids around the world.

TO DO:

1. On the next page, you'll find several links to weekly polls designed just for kids. Visit the sites to see which question best fits your curriculum or students' age group.

2. First, introduce the topic to your class. If necessary, share any background information that would help them understand the controversy.

3. Hold a preliminary vote with your students. Divide the class into groups, depending on how they voted.

4. Have the class debate, with each group providing one fact or opinion at a time. During the debate, allow students to change their minds and move from one group to another.

5. Hold a final vote, and tally the votes on the board. Determine the percentage for each vote and create a pie chart showing the results.

6. Create a "polling booth" at your computer. Access the online poll, and have each student click on his or her choice. (If you are participating in the Scholastic News Zone Poll, you can enter the number of boys and girls who voted for each choice.)

7. When you've finished, see the online results of the poll. Create a pie chart showing the results of kids around the country. How did these results compare with the class votes?

SITES TO GET STARTED..

Scholastic News Zone Poll
http://teacher.scholastic.com/newszone/poll/index.asp

Decisions, Decisions Online
http://www.teachtsp2.com/ddonline

Yahooligans/History Channel Weekly Poll
http://www.yahooligans.com/historychannel

ACTIVITY 4

Make Your Voice Heard!

SUBJECT AREA: Social Studies, Language Arts

OVERVIEW: Encourage your students to be active citizens by contacting government leaders about issues that matter to kids. They can take action immediately—it just takes a passionate, well-organized letter and a click of the mouse!

TO DO:

1. Which issues do your students care most about? Invite students to discuss issues or problems that have come up in

class or in the news that they wish they could do something about. These issues may range from the environment to endangered animals to homeless children. Write each issue on the board and take a quick class survey to select three topics that interest your students most.

2. Divide students into three groups and assign each group an issue to research. (The sites on the following page may be a good starting place to learn more about issues that affect kids, as well as specific actions they can take.) Encourage students to find the different causes of the problem. What are the real facts behind the issue? What are different solutions? Why might some people be opposed to a particular solution? Which solution would they choose? Have each group present their issue to the class.

3. Ask students to brainstorm ways in which people might influence these problems, such as raise money for a cause, take action in their own community, vote for different political leaders, or try to influence current leaders. Ask the class why government leaders listen to their constituents. Why might they listen to what kids think? Which might make a bigger difference—one letter or 100 letters?

4. Ask students to choose one of the issues they have researched. Who might be able to influence this issue? The President? Their representatives in Congress? The president of a company? (Most organizations that encourage people to write in support of or against an issue will provide the appropriate names and addresses to contact.) Students can find e-mail and postal addresses for the President and members of Congress at the "Contacting Congress" site on the next page.

5. Have each member of the class write a letter to the person or people they have chosen. Encourage students to use the facts they researched to support their opinions in a clear, concise, well-organized letter. Their passion should come through in their letter, but students should remain respectful. Each letter should include the student's name, school, address, city, and state. And of course, make sure students carefully check their letters for spelling and grammar.

6. Open "postal stations" at your computers and have students type and send their e-mails individually.

SITES TO GET STARTED......................................

Contacting Congress
http://www.congress.org

World Wildlife Fund
http://www.worldwildlife.org

United States Fund for UNICEF
http://www.unicefusa.org

Envirofacts Warehouse: U.S. EPA Student Center
http://www.epa.gov/students/envirofacts_warehouse.htm

ACTIVITY 5

Make New Friends and Explore a Different Community With a Partner Class

SUBJECT AREA: All

OVERVIEW: Partner with a "keypal" class and discover what life is like in a different state or country. Students in both classes can exchange information about everyday life, from weather conditions to local traditions, in their own hometowns.

TO DO:

1. Use one of the Web sites on the following page to find a "keypal" or partner class that matches your grade level.

2. E-mail the teacher to make sure you have the same general curriculum goals and time-commitment expectations. For example, will you plan cross-curricular lessons? Do you both agree to one project and e-mail exchange every week?

3. Set a schedule of activities. Here are a few ideas to get you started:

■ **MONTH 1:** Begin with a "Mystery City" game, in which classes exchange clues about their town's history, geography, landmarks, famous citizens, or weather. Each class must solve the clues to figure out where their partner students live!

■ **MONTH 2:** Set up a weather station and collect data

about the temperature, precipitation, and air pressure over a weeklong period. Exchange the data and compare the conditions between the two cities. Discuss how they are different and why.

▣ **MONTH 3:** Compare the costs of everyday items between the two towns. For example, create a "grocery receipt" that includes the cost of milk, eggs, Oreos, bread, and apples—as well as local sales tax. Include any items that may be grown locally, such as oranges. Do they cost more or less in your partner's town? Create a bar graph to show any differences in costs.

▣ **MONTH 4:** Pair students at similar levels and have a "math challenge." Students in one class begin by e-mailing word problems to their partners. Their partners must solve the problem, and send a new word problem along with their answer.

▣ **MONTH 5:** Send holiday greetings to your partner class. Describe the different holidays your students are celebrating and include any local or family traditions. Share any hopes and dreams students have for the new year.

▣ **MONTH 6:** Challenge your students' writing and comprehension abilities with a "secret garden" exchange. Invite each student to draw and color his or her own imaginary garden, which could include objects such as trees, flowers, a swing set, a few animals, a pond, or a wall. Next, have students write descriptions of their gardens with as much detail as possible. Exchange these descriptions with your partner class, and challenge the partner students to draw the secret gardens using the descriptions. Have students exchange the drawings of their secret gardens by e-mailing or mailing the images. Were the two drawings similar? How could the descriptions have been more vivid?

SITES TO GET STARTED.......................................

ePALS Classroom Exhange
http://www.epals.com

Kidscom: Find a Key Pal
http://www.kidscom.com/orakc/keypal/teachers/index.html

· ·

ACTIVITY 6

Get Published on the Web

SUBJECT AREA: Language Arts, Social Studies

OVERVIEW: There's nothing quite as motivating for kids as seeing their own work in print—and the Web is a great place to get started. Suddenly, kids are writing not just for teachers and other classmates, but for a worldwide audience! Several sites are dedicated to sharing student writing and artwork, but most are fairly selective about which works they will publish online. One way to involve all students in the process is by creating an in-class magazine of everyone's work. Then have the class select their favorite works to submit to the student-writing Web site.

TO DO:

1. Choose the writing genre that fits your current curriculum—such as news writing, creative stories, or poems—as well as the Web site where you'd like to submit students' work. Introduce different examples of this genre to your students.

2. Have a class discussion about the different places where you might see a writer's work in this genre—such as in magazines, newspapers, books, and even on the Web. Discuss some of the criteria for being published and keep a running list on the bulletin board. For example, the content or ideas should be new or interesting to readers; it should be exciting to read; it should be clearly written or well-organized; there should be no spelling or grammar mistakes.

3. Inform students that they will have two opportunities to publish their work: in a class magazine and on a Web site just for kids' work. Explain that in order to be published in the class magazine, students' work should meet the criteria the class has discussed. Then students will vote which stories or poems from the magazine will be submitted to the Web site. Remind them that not every writer gets his or her work published in magazines, newspapers, or books. Sometimes even the most talented writers have their work rejected.

4. Before students begin writing, you may want to share

examples of student writings that have been published online. Have the class talk about why these works may have been selected for the site.

5. After students have written their first drafts, have them work in pairs and edit their partner's work. Encourage students to use the checklist of criteria as they evaluate their partner's work.

6. Once students have revised—and perhaps illustrated— their work, create an in-class magazine. Invite students to come up with a name for the magazine. Getting published in the class magazine gives every student a feeling of accomplishment, even if his or her work isn't submitted to the Web site.

7. Let every student read his or her own writing aloud and have the class vote on their favorite pieces. Finally, submit the class's top five choices to the Web site you selected.

SITES TO GET STARTED...

Children's Express World Wide
http://www.cenews.org

KidNews
http://www.KidNews.com

KidAuthors
http://www.kidauthors.com/default.asp

ZuZu
http://www.zuzu.org

Poetry Pals
http://www.geocities.com/EnchantedForest/5165/index1.html

ACTIVITY 7

Go on an Internet Scavenger Hunt

SUBJECT AREA: All

OVERVIEW: No matter what topic you're teaching, you'll find a wealth of resources on the Internet to support your curriculum. With an Internet Scavenger Hunt, you can send students to the best sites on the Web to collect information in an organized and fun activity. To get you started, we've provided a "Wild Weather" Scavenger Hunt on page 50.

TO DO:

1. Create an Internet Scavenger Hunt that features the best, most appropriate Web sites that match your curriculum theme. Develop specific questions that challenge kids to find important facts on each site. As an incentive, make a game out of the Scavenger Hunt answers. For example, answers could be found in a word search, used to solve a riddle or complete a crossword puzzle.

2. Hand out copies of the Internet Scavenger Hunt. (See page 50 for a sample.)

3. Have students work in small groups to research answers to the questions online.

4. Challenge different teams to create their own Scavenger Hunts for the rest of the class. You should provide the theme and the general sites to visit, and let students create the game!

Answers to Wild Weather Scavenger Hunt

1. Alley 2. Texas 3. counterclockwise 4. severe 5. eye
6. Arthur 7. tropical 8. Hugo **Riddle:** The ocean

Wild Weather Scavenger Hunt

Directions: Visit the sites below to learn about hurricanes and
tornadoes. Use the facts at each site to fill in the blank. When
you're done, rearrange the letters in the brackets to solve the riddle.

Tornadoes

1. Most tornadoes occur in "Tornado [__] __ __ __ __," an area in the central
U.S. stretching from Nebraska to Texas.
http://whyfiles.news.wisc.edu/013tornado/tornado_main1.html

2. The state with the highest average number of tornadoes a year is
[__] __ __ __ __
http://www.ncdc.noaa.gov/ol/climate/severeweather/small/avgt5095.gif

3. Tornadoes are powerful funnels of spiraling winds. A tornado in the United
States would probably rotate in a
__ __ __ [__] __ __ __ __ __ __ __ __ __ __ __
direction.
http://www.txdirect.net/~msattler/tornado.htm

4. Scientists use the Fujita Scale to measure the power of a tornado. A tornado
with 200-mile-an-hour winds is considered __ __ __ [__] __ __.
http://whyfiles.news.wisc.edu/013tornado/tornado_main2.html

Hurricanes

5. The __ __ [__] of a hurricane is the calm area in the center of the storm.
http://www.txdirect.net/~msattler/hurrican.htm

6. The first hurricane of the year 2002 will be named
__ __ __ [__] __ __.
http://www.miamisci.org/hurricane/hurricanenames.html

7. Hurricanes form over warm, __ __ __ __ __ [__] __ __ oceans.
http://www.miamisci.org/hurricane/howhurrwork.html

8. Hurricane __ __ __ [__] hit the coast of South Carolina in 1989.
http://www.ncdc.noaa.gov/ol/climate/severeweather/2hur8196.gif

Riddle

Unscramble the circled letters above to solve the riddle:
What doesn't get any wetter, no matter how much it rains?

__ __ __ __ __ __ __ __ __

Sites You Should Not Miss

Language Arts

Booklist
http://www.ala.org/booklist/index.html

> This digital counterpart of the American Library Association's *Booklist* magazine posts reviews and information about new books and other media for young, middle-school, and older children.

The Children's Literature Web Guide
http://www.acs.ucalgary.ca/~dkbrown/index.html

> Online stories, kids' writing, and information about books, authors, book awards, and storytelling.

Internet Public Library Author Page
http://www.ipl.org/youth/AskAuthor

> Features biographies of some favorite children's authors, as well as their answers to kids' questions. Includes links to authors' and illustrators' Web sites.

Kidz Page
http://web.aimnet.com/~veeceet/kids/kidzpage.html

> Part of this Web site presents a selection of rib-tickling poems from writers like Ogden Nash and Lewis Carroll. But most of this site is dedicated to poems written by kids. Includes guidelines for submitting poetry.

Literature Online Collection
http://www.csun.edu/~vceed009/lalit.html

A comprehensive list of links to various works of literature, as well as to author sites and online bookstores.

MidLink Magazine
http://longwood.cs.ucf.edu/~MidLink/index.html

This online, digital magazine "for kids by kids from 8 to 18" invites article submissions from classrooms around the world. Project announcements inform you of upcoming topics so you can plan your curriculum accordingly.

SCORE CyberGuides
http://www.sdcoe.k12.ca.us/score/cyberguide.html

You'll find this collection of interactive Web activities extremely useful in your language-arts curriculum. The activities are literature-based and meet the California State Standards.

Wacky Web Tales
http://www.eduplace.com/tales/index.html

In this online version of Mad Libs, kids can create their own wacky stories, as well as submit new story ideas for other kids to play with.

Word Central
http://www.wordcentral.com

Sponsored by Merriam-Webster, this online-dictionary site offers more than just word definitions. Check out the Daily Buzz Word to learn a new word, and build your own personal dictionary.

Writing With Writers
http://teacher.scholastic.com/writewit/index.htm

Join these exclusive writing seminars with famous writers, such as Virginia Hamilton and Jack Prelutsky. Get tips on how to write biographies, folktales, poetry, and more!

Vocabulary.com
http://www.vocabulary.com

Vocabulary University offers fun and interactive word puzzles to help build students' vocabulary.

Math

Ask Dr. Math
http://mathforum.com/dr.math

Students e-mail their math questions to Dr. Math—actually a team of math experts from around the world. The "doctor" responds via e-mail and posts answers on bulletin boards.

Blue Dog Can Count!
http://kao.ini.cmu.edu:5550/bdf.html

The character Blue Dog will bark the answer to addition, subtraction, multiplication, and other math problems at this site.

Elementary Problem of the Week
http://mathforum.com/elempow

Part of the Math Forum, "this project is designed to challenge elementary students with nonroutine problems, and to encourage them to verbalize their solutions."

Flashcards for Kids
http://www.edu4kids.com/math

Online flashcards with a variety of mathematical puzzles to help build kids' skills.

MathMagic!
http://mathforum.com/mathmagic

At this site, students from paired schools work together to come up with solutions to posted problems. If a class doesn't want to participate in the full program, students can still read and solve posted problems without registering.

Math Problems of the Week
http://www.mbnet.mb.ca/~jfinch/math.html

One math problem each week for grades 3 to 4 and grades 5 to 6.

The Money Game
http://www.moneygame.com

The Money Game is set up for schools, with students taking on the role of investment managers. The game itself is rewarding and fun, and the class with the best investments over three months wins a prize.

Science and Technology

4,000 Years of Women in Science
http://www.astr.ua.edu/4000WS

> This site lists more than 125 names from our scientific and technical past—and they're all female!

Bill Nye the Science Guy
http://nyelabs.kcts.org/flash_go.html

> Bill Nye applies his entertaining approach to science to the Web, with a Demo of the Day, highlights from the day's television episode, and a chance to e-mail your own query.

Calculating Machines
http://www.webcom.com/calc

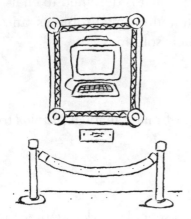

> Learn the history of calculating devices from the abacus to electric calculators of the 1950s. Includes biographies of some inventors, photos, and descriptions of various devices.

The Computer Museum Network
http://www.tcm.org/html/history/timeline/index.html

> This site contains a wealth of computer activities and applications. Students can browse a historical timeline of important events and people in computer history from 1945 to the present. Includes access to interactive exhibits, a resource list, and educational materials that can be adapted for classroom use.

Dinosauria On-line
http://www.dinosauria.com

> This technical site on dinosaurs comes complete with pictures, maps, discussions about dinosaur anatomy and family tree, and more. Dictionaries and maps provide definitions of important terms, a listing of known genera, and other interesting information.

Discovery Online: Science Live!
http://www.discovery.com/news/sciencelive/sciencelive.html

> Get the latest on medicine, space, animals, cutting-edge technology, and other science news—if it's science and in the news, chances are you'll find it here.

Exploring Planets in the Classroom
http://www.soest.hawaii.edu/SPACEGRANT/class_acts

> At this site, you'll find more than 25 hands-on science activities

54

for both teachers and students wishing to explore geology, earth, and planetary sciences.

Hall of Ideas
http://www.lucent.com/minds/gallery

Set up as an online gallery, this site features scientific break-throughs and technological milestones accomplished by Bell Laboratories, from high-fidelity recording in 1925 to a 1993 personal-computer video system.

The Invention Dimension
http://web.mit.edu/invent

Go to this information resource to learn more about American inventors and their discoveries. Features an inventor of the week, surveys, and links to other sites about inventors and inventions.

The Learning Web at the U.S. Geological Survey
http://www.usgs.gov/education/index.html

Visit "Teaching in the Learning Web" to find a collection of educational resources you can use in the classroom. "Living in the Learning Web" offers topics about conditions on Earth that affect people every day and everywhere.

Make Your Own Seismogram!
http://quake.geo.berkeley.edu/bdsn/make_seismogram.html

You'll get all the parameters you need to create a seismo-graph. Includes instructions, maps, and sample (real) seismograms from previous earthquakes. Choose from stations all over California and plot your own parameters. This also provides an access point for current information about earthquake activity around the world.

Marie Curie
http://www.xray.hmc.psu.edu/rci/ss4/ss4_11.html

Learn about the life of Marie Curie and her scientific contributions as shown through a series of postage stamps from countries around the world. The site also features other postage stamps that provide a philatelic history of radiation, complete with images of the stamps and background text.

National Earthquake Information Center: Earthquake Bulletin
http://gldss7.cr.usgs.gov/neis/qed/qed.html

This site provides up-to-date information on the date, time,

latitude, longitude, and magnitude of recent earthquakes around the world. It also locates those earthquakes on a series of maps.

Newton's Apple Index
http://ericir.syr.edu/Projects/Newton

This companion site to *Newton's Apple* on PBS features comprehensive lesson plans that supplement the TV show. Best of all, you don't need to watch the show to benefit from the site.

Triumph of the Nerds: A History of the Computer
http://www.pbs.org/nerds/timeline/index.html

Don't miss "A History of Computers" in this PBS companion site to the program *Triumph of the Nerds.* This historical timeline is divided into six sections: Prehistory (3000 B.C.), Electronics, Mini, Micro, Networks, and WWW. Information is presented in a concise format, rich with graphics, pictures, and maps.

Tsunami!
http://www.geophys.washington.edu/tsunami/welcome.html

This detailed site contains extensive background information about tsunamis, including how they form and travel, and what impact they have on people. Includes up-to-date research and survey data about recent tsunamis.

The Why Files
http://whyfiles.news.wisc.edu

The Why Files explores the science behind the news. Its bimonthly issues focus on the science (and math, engineering, and technology) of everyday life, from outer space to microbiology to the statistics of political polling.

Social Studies and History

Adventure Online
http://www.adventureonline.com/index.html

Students participate in modern-day explorations and voyages to Central America, Africa, and other places around the world. They also get to communicate with the adventurers doing the actual traveling. Records and photographs from previous trips continue to provide learning resources for the classroom, even after the adventure is over in real time.

Amazon Interactive

http://www.eduweb.com/amazon.html

Explore the geography of the Ecuadorian Amazon through online games and activities. Learn about the rain forest and the Quichua people who call it home. Then try your hand at running a community-based ecotourism project along the Río Napo.

Architecture in America

http://lcweb2.loc.gov/detroit/archamer.html

Containing 40 photographs, which have been selected from the Detroit Publishing Company collection, this site examines how changes brought about by the Civil War, industrialization, and westward expansion affected American architecture. The photos, flanked by text, show all types of buildings, from private homes to skyscrapers.

Biography

http://www.biography.com

The heart of this site is a searchable online collection of 15,000 cross-referenced biographies. The site also provides the full text of selected opening chapters and reviews of best-selling biographies, as well as schedules of upcoming episodes of the TV program *Biography* on A&E.

Distinguished Women of Past and Present

http://www.DistinguishedWomen.com

A collection of biographies of female writers, educators, scientists, heads of state, politicians, civil-rights crusaders, artists, entertainers, and others.

End of the Oregon Trail

http://www.teleport.com/~eotic/index.html

This site, maintained by a living-history museum in Oregon, focuses on the history of the Oregon Trail. It describes the covered wagons, provisions packed for the difficult trip, and the many routes of the trail. Includes teaching ideas and links to other related sites.

Famous Hispanics in the World and History

http://coloquio.com/famosos/alpha.html

An extensive list of links to biographies of important Hispanic men and women.

George Washington's Mount Vernon

http://www.mountvernon.org

This site gives all the information you would ever want about Mount Vernon, including photos, maps, biographical information, and news of current archaeological excavations, as well as tourist information.

The Great Adventure

http://www.cmcc.muse.digital.ca/cmc/cmceng/childeng.html

This interactive site features a virtual museum tour. With the click of a mouse, students can get a glimpse of life in various countries around the world. Text is available in English or French.

The History Net: Where History Lives on the Web

http://www.thehistorynet.com

Access magazine articles, diaries, photographs, and interviews on this site. Visit the battlefields of the Civil War or read about the adventures of a Russian pilot who fought on three fronts. Test your history knowledge with a daily quiz, or find out what happened on this day in history.

Holidays on the Net

http://www.holidays.net

This highly interactive site explores the history and traditions of ethnic, religious, and cultural holidays celebrated in the United States, including Father's and Mother's days, and Martin Luther King Jr. Day.

Kids of the Web

http://www.wenet.net/~leroyc/kidsweb/index.html

This is one of the largest collections of links to home pages of kids around the world.

Lower East Side Tenement Museum

http://www.wnet.org/tenement

This totally interactive site depicts life in a New York City tenement from 1870 to 1915. Click on the windows of the tenement to witness vignettes of day-to-day life, presented graphically with accompanying text.

Martin Luther King Jr.: The King Center

http://www.thekingcenter.com

The King Center in Atlanta is a "living memorial" to Dr. King. It includes exhibits as well as programs to promote King's vision of nonviolent change. This Web site describes the center and its history, its diverse programs, and its research facilities.

Mount Rushmore: The Four Most Famous Guys in Rock
http://www.state.sd.us/state/executive/tourism/rushmore/index.htm

This site is a rich source of information on Mount Rushmore, complete with photos and text.

Timeline of the American Civil Rights Movement
http://www.wmich.edu/politics/mlk

This site is structured around a timeline of nine events in the civil-rights movement, from the 1954 *Brown* v. *Board of Education* Supreme Court decision to the 1965 Selma-to-Montgomery march in Alabama. Each event includes graphics and descriptive text, as well as links to primary historical documents.

Titanic Historical Society
http://www.titanic1.org

Far from the ocean in landlocked western Massachusetts, this unique, privately owned display in the Henry's Jewelry building is dedicated to the ill-fated liner. This site includes a wide range of information on the *Titanic*.

Today in History
http://lcweb2.loc.gov/ammem/today/today.html

The Library of Congress began a day-by-day listing of historical events on April 1, 1997. Search the archive for the day of your choice.

United Nations Headquarters Online Tour
http://www.un.org/Overview/Tours/UNHQ

This definitive site takes viewers on a virtual tour of the United Nations headquarters in New York City. Through images and text, you can find out about the goals of the United Nations.

A Virtual Tour of Plymouth Plantation
http://pilgrims.net/plymouth

Plymouth (Plimoth) Plantation was the first permanent European settlement in southern New England. This online tour uses exhibits from the modern-day re-creation of this settlement to explore life in the 1620s.

Welcome to the Biographical Dictionary
http://s9.com/biography

This dictionary contains concise biographical data on more than 18,000 people from ancient times to the present. Information includes birth and death years, professions, positions held, literary and artistic works and other achievements. The dictionary is all text.

The White House for Kids
http://www.whitehouse.gov/WH/kids/html/kidshome.html

This site is divided into three sections: a tour of the White House, historic moments of the presidency, and "Inside the White House," a newsletter for young people. Children are invited to write the President from this site.

Teacher Resources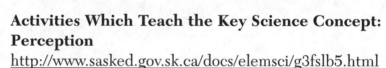

100th Day of School Activities
http://www.globalclassroom.org/100days.html

At this site, you will find suggestions for celebrating the 100th day of school from teachers around the world. Many of the lesson plans are math-related (including ideas for math key-pals), but there are several interdisciplinary ideas as well.

Activities Which Teach the Key Science Concept: Perception
http://www.sasked.gov.sk.ca/docs/elemsci/g3fslb5.html

This site is one part of the much larger "Evergreen Curriculum," Saskatchewan's elementary science curriculum for grades K–6. This particular page contains a wide range of activities, experiments, and lesson plans for teaching the science of sound at the elementary level. Curriculum materials for many other science topics can be found by using the navigation arrows from this page.

Ask ERIC
http://ericir.syr.edu

Ask ERIC is the card catalogue of the Internet—a listing of thousands of educational articles as well as lesson plans from CNN, NASA, and PBS, to name a few. A brief summary is given, along with information on how to get the entire text either electronically or through a local library. You can search the database for grant information, lesson plans, journal articles, and much more. You can also ask questions via e-mail and get free help from ERIC experts.

Content Knowledge: A Compendium of Standards and Benchmarks for K–12 Education
http://www.mcrel.org/standards-benchmarks

The authors of this report have analyzed the standards and benchmarks from a variety of national reports in every curriculum area and consolidated them into one source for searching or browsing.

Discovery Channel Online
http://www.discovery.com

This huge site presents special events and features relating to stories covered on cable TV's Discovery Channel, and covers hundreds of topics. You also can tap the site's vast resource of past stories, on topics ranging from little-known inventors to daily life in Bosnia. You can search a subject of interest, check out TV schedules, chat live, or post messages on topical bulletin boards.

Education Week on the Web
http://www.edweek.com

Online news from the world of education

Exploratorium ExploraNet
http://www.exploratorium.edu

This San Francisco-based interactive museum of science, art, and human perception brings some of its exhibits online, and also offers teacher resources, book lists, recommended sites, and interdisciplinary materials.

K–12 Resources for Teachers and Students
http://www.cnidr.org/k12.html

This hub site provides searching mechanisms and links to selected Web sites for educators.

National Assessment of Educational Progress
http://www.ed.gov/NCES/naep

Focusing on recent reports of the National Assessment of Educational Progress (NAEP), this site aims to analyze and evaluate education in the U.S. (and other countries) in order to facilitate improvements and provide educational information for parents, teachers, educators, and others. From this site, you can see summaries and download whole copies of the reports.

Teachers Helping Teachers

http://www.pacificnet.net/~mandel

This site is the place for teachers to exchange teaching tips and ideas from lesson plans to bulletin-board ideas to integrating special-needs students in the classroom. Includes resources, links, and even stress-reduction tips.

ThinkQuest

http://www.thinkquest.org

ThinkQuest is an annual contest that challenges students, ages 12 to 19, "to use the Internet as a collaborative, interactive teaching and learning tool." Take a look at some of the wonderful winning sites!

Resources for Math Teachers

http://www.ucs.mun.ca/~mathed/t/T-index.html

This site, written especially for teachers, includes five lessons designed to teach students about transformations. Brief lesson summaries for each activity are given, as well as worksheets for student use. Small samples of some Escher works are included.

Young Children

The Crayola Home Page

http://www.crayola.com

Everything you always wanted to know about crayons.

Little Explorers

http://www.EnchantedLearning.com/Dictionary.html

Click on a letter of the alphabet and connect to lots of pictures of words that begin with that letter, and hot links to Web sites about each word.

Sesame Street Central

http://www.ctw.org/sesame

On this kids-activities page, play games with friends from *Sesame Street:* Prairie Dawn, Elmo, and the Cookie Monster.

Afterword

Wow! The Internet is really incredible. And it has been around only since 1994. Imagine what we'll be doing with it in just a few years. Sometimes the size and power of the Internet can be overwhelming. As you begin to use the Internet in your classroom, here's something to keep in mind on your cyber-travels:

You need support. Most people don't master using the Internet on their own. Fortunately, there are helpful resources all around you. Tap your friends and colleagues for great Web sites they've found that improve their teaching and their lives. Your technology coordinator at school will also have valuable knowledge. If you need help on a subject that no one around you is familiar with, turn to the Internet itself. The right discussion groups can usually find the answer to almost any query. Remember: One of the best ways to find fantastic stuff on the Internet is to just start clicking.

Most important, acknowledge the learning curve. No one is born an expert, and no one is ever done learning. With the vast amount of information out there, be patient with yourself as you start to learn where the good stuff is and how you can get to it.

Notes